MEDICAL BREAKTHROUGHS
VACCINES

A GRAPHIC HISTORY

PAIGE V. POLINSKY

ILLUSTRATED BY DANTE GINEVRA

GRAPHIC UNIVERSE™ • MINNEAPOLIS

Graphic Universe™
An imprint of Lerner Publishing Group, Inc.
241 First Avenue North
Minneapolis, MN 55401 USA

For reading levels and more information, look up this title at www.lernerbooks.com.

Main body text is set in Dave Gibbons Lower. Typeface provided by Comicraft.

Library of Congress Cataloging-in-Publication Data

Names: Polinsky, Paige V., author. | Ginevra, Dante, 1976- illustrator.
Title: Vaccines : a graphic history / Paige V. Polinsky ; illustrations by Dante Ginevra.
Description: Minneapolis : Graphic Universe, [2022] | Series: Medical breakthroughs |
    Includes bibliographical references and index. | Audience: Ages 8–12 | Audience:
    Grades 4–6 | Summary: "Vaccines safely introduce the body to diseases, which helps
    people fight them later on. Early vaccinations took place centuries ago. Doctors
    across nations took up the fight, developing vaccines for diseases from smallpox to
    COVID-19"— Provided by publisher.
Identifiers: LCCN 2021014450 (print) | LCCN 2021014451 (ebook) | ISBN 9781541583900
    (library binding) | ISBN 9781728448725 (paperback) | ISBN 9781728444147 (ebook)
Subjects: LCSH: Vaccines—Juvenile literature. | Vaccination—Juvenile literature.
Classification: LCC RA638 .P64 2022 (print) | LCC RA638 (ebook) | DDC 614.4/7—dc23

LC record available at https://lccn.loc.gov/2021014450
LC ebook record available at https://lccn.loc.gov/2021014451

Manufactured in the United States of America
1 – CG – 12/15/21

TABLE OF CONTENTS

CHAPTER 1:
ANTIBODY BUILDING

Your body works hard to keep itself healthy. If it recognizes dangerous viruses or bacteria, it creates proteins called antibodies to fight those germs. This is called immunity.

Passive immunity comes from a human or animal donor. A mother passes antibodies to her unborn baby through the placenta. Once the baby is born, it receives antibodies through breast milk.

Passive immunity is important. But it lasts a few months at most after a baby is born. So, a baby can only fight infection this way for a brief period of time. After that, the body needs extra help to stay healthy.

Vaccines safely introduce your immune system to diseases. That allows your body to recognize a disease later on and create antibodies to fight it. This is called active immunity.

Most childhood vaccinations are completed between birth and the age of six. Many happen more than once or in combinations.

You'll come back for a booster shot in about a year.

Vaccines are some of the safest and most effective medicines available. Many dangerous diseases have been reduced or eliminated thanks to vaccines.

Different vaccines work in different ways.

Live-attenuated vaccines use a weakened version of the disease-causing germ.

Varicella (chicken pox)

Inactivated vaccines use a version of the germ killed by heat or chemicals.

Influenza (flu)

Subunit vaccines use specific pieces of the germ.

Pertussis (whooping cough)

Toxoid vaccines use a toxin made by the germ.

Tetanus

Some vaccines may cause soreness or swelling around the site of the injection. They may also cause a fever. These reactions mean your body is learning to fight the disease.

Soon you'll be stronger than ever.

Vaccines save up to three million lives each year. They are our best weapon against disease. It took many scientists and many decades to develop them.

CHAPTER 2:
THE SPECKLED MONSTER

For centuries, the smallpox virus was one of the world's deadliest diseases. In some areas, it threatened entire populations.

By the 1500s, written accounts from Asia were reporting a method to combat smallpox.

It often involved collecting scabs from smallpox pustules. Doctors crushed the scabs into a powder. They used the powder to infect healthy people. Infection from the weakened virus often led to immunity. This process later become known as inoculation.

The technique took longer to reach Europe. In the early 1700s, smallpox killed around 400,000 people across the continent every year. The disease was nicknamed the speckled monster.

At the time, doctors disagreed over how best to treat smallpox. Many fought the disease with cold air and bloodletting.

Cold treatment is the best thing for her. Cold and leeches.

Survivors often had deep scars. But they were also immune to the disease.

It's a wonder she's still here.

Thank goodness she can't catch it again.

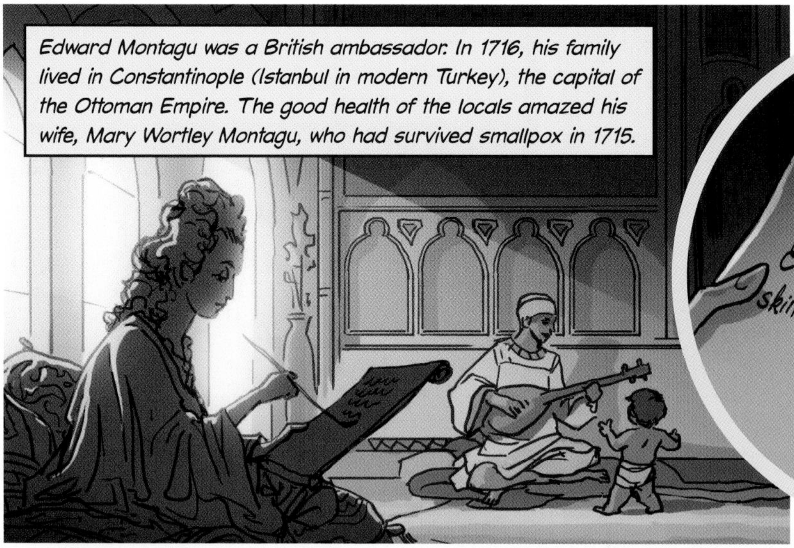
Edward Montagu was a British ambassador. In 1716, his family lived in Constantinople (Istanbul in modern Turkey), the capital of the Ottoman Empire. The good health of the locals amazed his wife, Mary Wortley Montagu, who had survived smallpox in 1715.

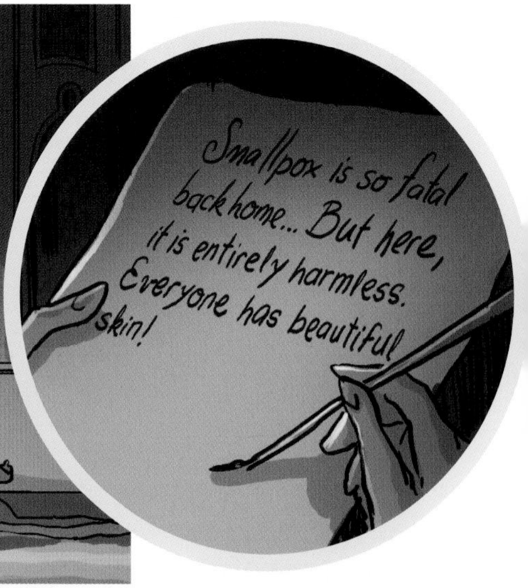
Smallpox is so fatal back home... But here, it is entirely harmless. Everyone has beautiful skin!

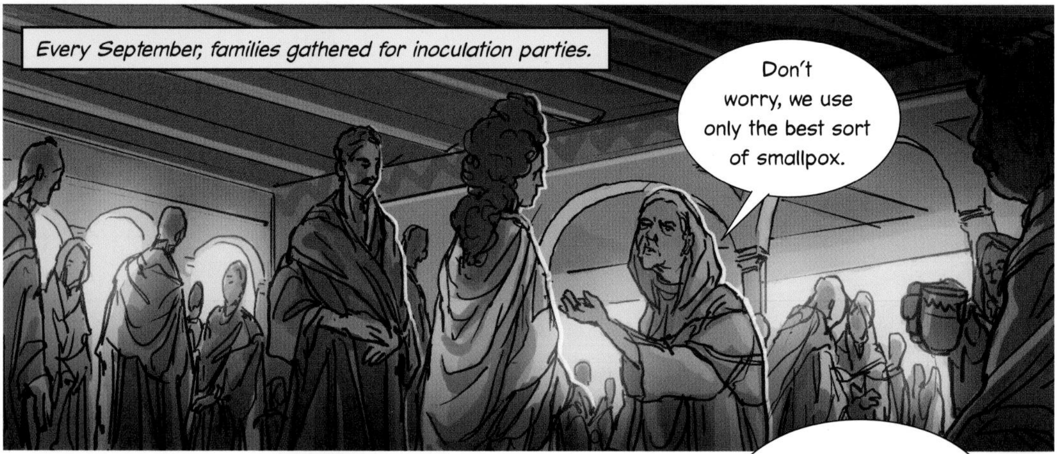
Every September, families gathered for inoculation parties.
Don't worry, we use only the best sort of smallpox.

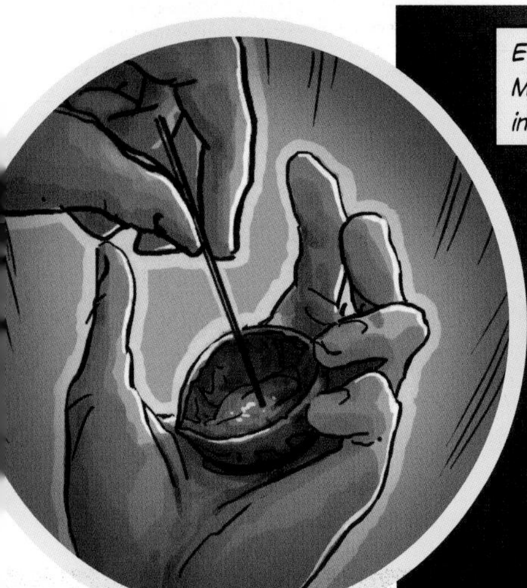

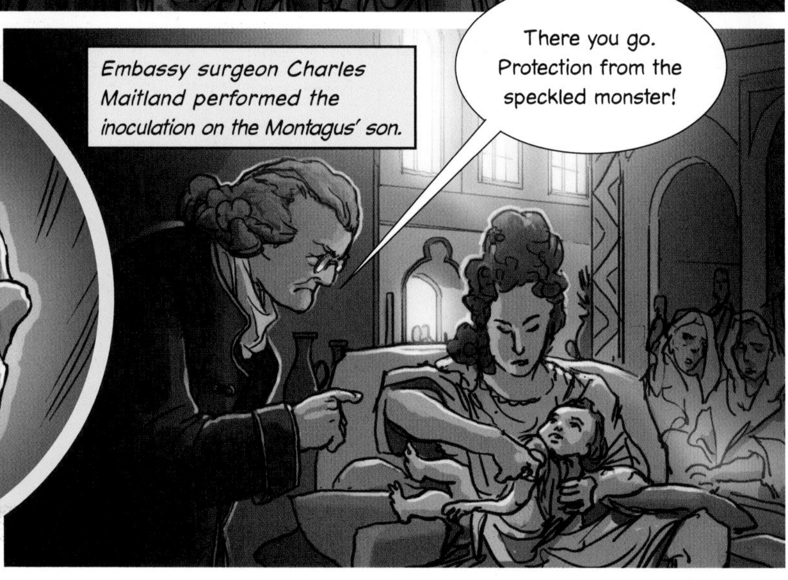
Embassy surgeon Charles Maitland performed the inoculation on the Montagus' son.
There you go. Protection from the speckled monster!

In 1718, the Montagus returned to London. Three years later, a fresh wave of smallpox hit London. Lady Montagu invited an audience to watch Maitland inoculate her daughter, Mary.

Today, we make history. You are about to witness the first such procedure in England!

Not everybody was convinced about the treatment.

Hocus pocus. That Lady Montagu has no medical training!

They will infect all of England before the week is out.

But a stream of visitors later came to witness the girl's recovery.

Perhaps there's something to it after all!

By 1723, smallpox inoculations had become commonplace in England. Meanwhile, a rumor spread between farmers and country doctors. Catching a mild virus called cowpox also seemed to cause smallpox immunity.

Did you hear 'bout Joan? She caught the smallpox. You should be careful.

Don't worry, I caught cowpox just last year. Everyone knows you can't catch smallpox if you've had cowpox.

In 1774, smallpox hit the English city of Dorset. Farmer Benjamin Jesty collected scabs from the udders of a cow with cowpox. Jesty gathered samples of the cowpox virus from the scabs.

An inoculation would have used the live smallpox virus. Instead, Jesty infected his family with the cowpox virus. This was much milder and safer.

Jesty did not know it, but he had performed the very first vaccination!

Word spread of Jesty's daring vaccinations. Twenty years later, English doctor Edward Jenner would bring this folk remedy into the medical spotlight.

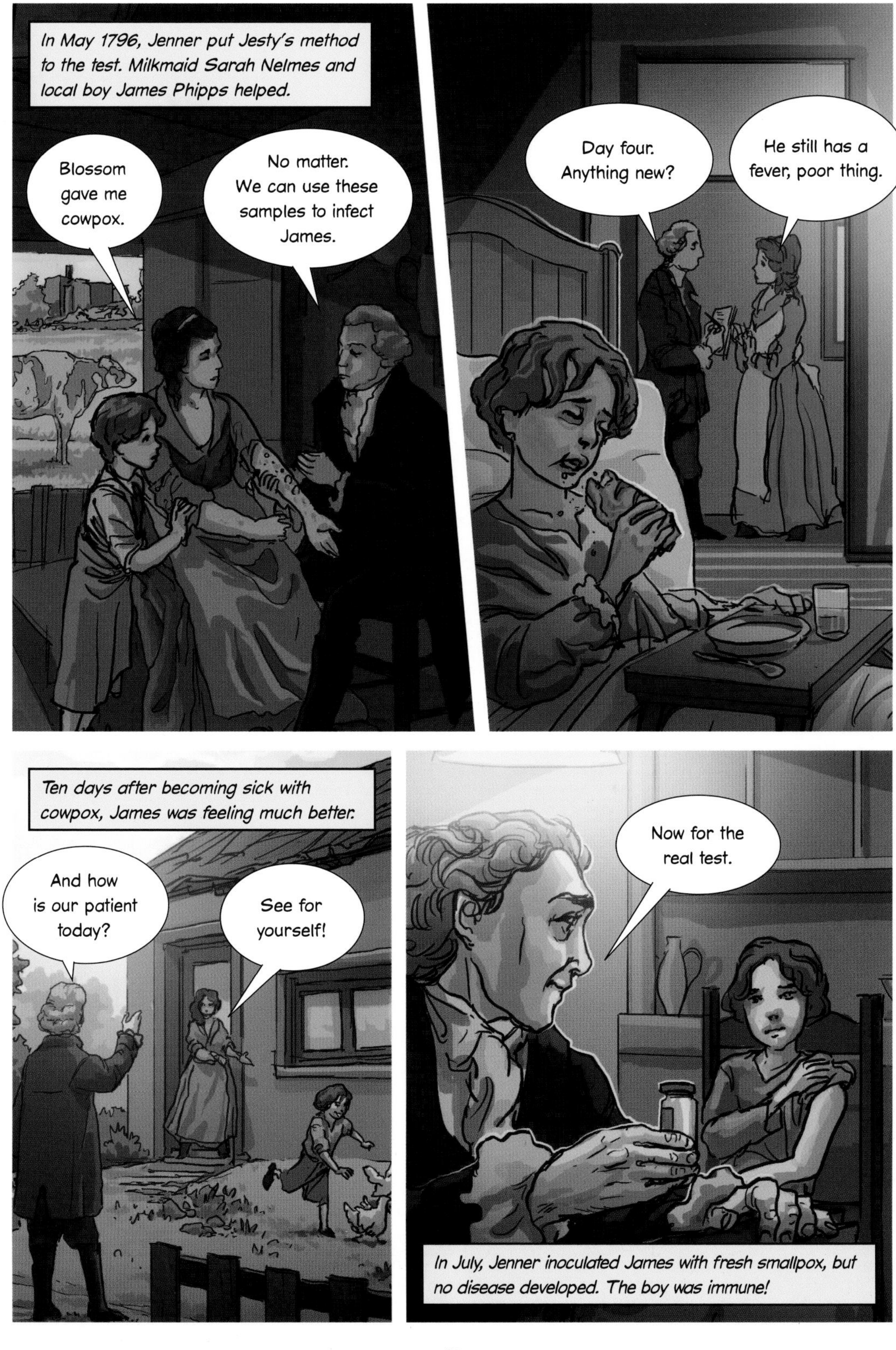
In May 1796, Jenner put Jesty's method to the test. Milkmaid Sarah Nelmes and local boy James Phipps helped.
Blossom gave me cowpox.
No matter. We can use these samples to infect James.
Day four. Anything new?
He still has a fever, poor thing.
Ten days after becoming sick with cowpox, James was feeling much better.
And how is our patient today?
See for yourself!
Now for the real test.
In July, Jenner inoculated James with fresh smallpox, but no disease developed. The boy was immune!

In 1798, Jenner published his findings on smallpox vaccination in a private booklet.

And you call this method vaccination?

Vacca . . . Oh, I see!

Indeed! After all, what is the Latin word for cow?

An Inquiry into the Causes and Effects of the Variolae Vaccinae

Slowly, word spread. Jenner sent vaccine materials to anyone who requested them.

He would devote his life to controlling disease through vaccination.

We can't offer you much in return . . .

I built this to help families like yours. You owe me nothing.

The Temple of Vaccinia

In 1800, Benjamin Waterhouse became the first US doctor to receive and test Jenner's materials. He used the vaccine on his son.

Daniel Oliver, my boy, you have just received the first vaccine in American history!

Waterhouse vaccinated his other children and several servants too. To test their immunity, he brought them to a smallpox hospital.

This young helper remains healthy! I must congratulate you, sir.

Waterhouse urged US Vice President Thomas Jefferson to introduce vaccines to Jefferson's home state of Virginia. Jefferson promised to spread the discovery across the nation.

Thank you for the pamphlet. Of all the medical discoveries, I know of none as valuable as this...

CHAPTER 3

DECADES OF DISCOVERY

The first lab-developed vaccine occurred in 1879. French chemist Louis Pasteur and his assistant, Charles Chamberland, were studying chicken cholera. This common disease could kill 90 percent of a farmer's flock.

Charles, please remember to inoculate the hens before you go on holiday.

Yes, yes. Hens. Of course.

Vacation, here I come!

One month later . . .

Er . . . better late than never?

Inoculating the hens with fresh cholera could have killed them. But the hens survived the month-old inoculations.

Their symptoms are so mild.

By aging the bacteria, we've weakened the disease!

Pasteur then exposed the same hens to fresh bacteria. They were immune!

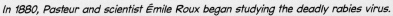
In 1880, Pasteur and scientist Émile Roux began studying the deadly rabies virus.

In July 1885, Joseph Meister and his mother came to the lab. A rabid dog had attacked Joseph.

We heard a scientist here is creating a rabies cure.

This vaccine is the weakest formula. We will use a stronger formula each day.

Pasteur and Roux had never tested their vaccine on humans. But it was the boy's only chance of survival.

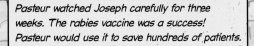
Pasteur watched Joseph carefully for three weeks. The rabies vaccine was a success! Pasteur would use it to save hundreds of patients.

Fifty years later, a different disease was on the rise. Between 1926 and 1930, pertussis (whooping cough) killed more than 36,000 people in the United States. Most victims were infants.

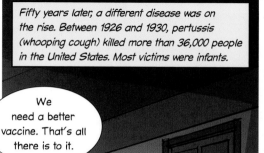

We need a better vaccine. That's all there is to it.

Michigan scientists Pearl Kendrick and Grace Eldering studied milk and water purity for the state. In 1932, they began developing their own whooping cough vaccine.

The lab can barely afford mice right now . . .

This disease is killing six thousand children every year. If we can stop it, I'll work for free.

Kendrick and Eldering worked long hours to study the disease. They collected bacteria samples from nearby homes.

At first, they had to create a custom vaccine for each person.

Later, Kendrick and Eldering weakened whooping cough bacteria with the chemical thimerosal. By 1933, they had developed a formula that would work for everybody.

We based the formula on several local strains of the disease.

Has it been tested?

Many times. Even on ourselves!

The next year, they began a controlled field study. A field study involves tests outside of the lab. When funds for the study ran low, the team called First Lady Eleanor Roosevelt for help.

What wonderful work! You have my full support.

The study ended in 1939 with exciting results. Vaccinated children were much more protected from whooping cough. By 1940, the vaccine was in use across the nation.

During the late 1940s, a frightening virus was causing panic in the United States. Poliomyelitis (polio) can damage the central nervous system. Major outbreaks were paralyzing 35,000 people each year.

These are some of our most severe cases. The patients can't breathe on their own.

The shell helps protect the sample from contamination.

In 1936, scientist Frank Macfarlane Burnet had discovered that chicken eggs offered the perfect environment for growing large amounts of certain viruses. He used eggs to grow and study the influenza virus.

But the polio virus was difficult to grow safely using eggs. Scientists could not mass produce the virus. This slowed vaccine development.

In 1948, scientists at Boston Children's Hospital used a new method. They found that the polio virus grew quickly in skin and muscle tissue from human embryos.

Thomas H. Weller

John F. Enders

Frederick C. Robbins

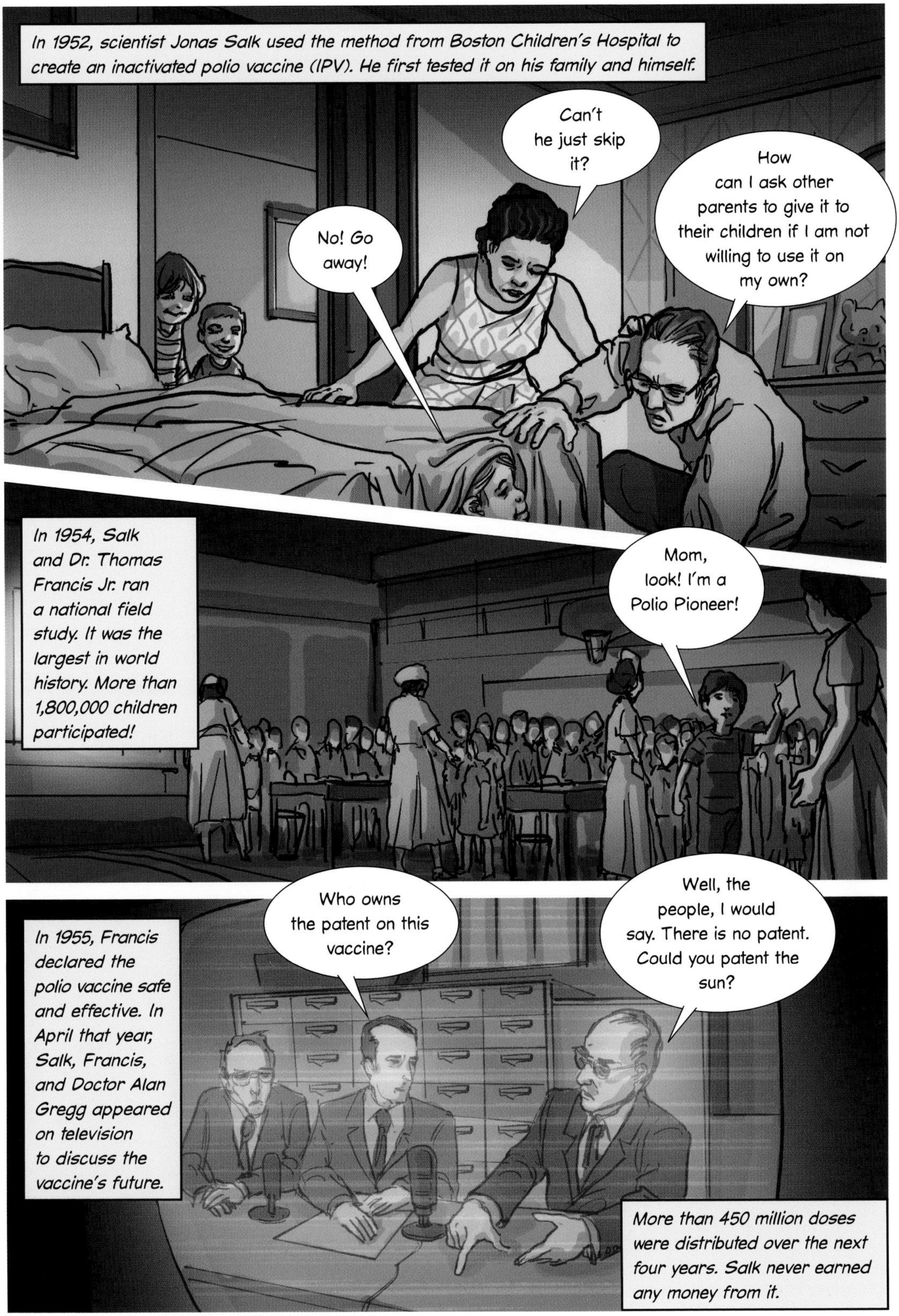
In 1952, scientist Jonas Salk used the method from Boston Children's Hospital to create an inactivated polio vaccine (IPV). He first tested it on his family and himself.
Can't he just skip it?
How can I ask other parents to give it to their children if I am not willing to use it on my own?
No! Go away!
In 1954, Salk and Dr. Thomas Francis Jr. ran a national field study. It was the largest in world history. More than 1,800,000 children participated!
Mom, look! I'm a Polio Pioneer!
In 1955, Francis declared the polio vaccine safe and effective. In April that year, Salk, Francis, and Doctor Alan Gregg appeared on television to discuss the vaccine's future.
Who owns the patent on this vaccine?
Well, the people, I would say. There is no patent. Could you patent the sun?
More than 450 million doses were distributed over the next four years. Salk never earned any money from it.

By the 1960s, vaccine development was progressing quickly. But certain diseases still harmed the nation.

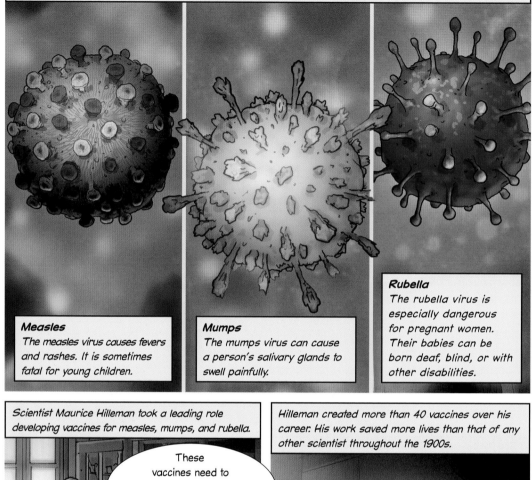

Measles
The measles virus causes fevers and rashes. It is sometimes fatal for young children.

Mumps
The mumps virus can cause a person's salivary glands to swell painfully.

Rubella
The rubella virus is especially dangerous for pregnant women. Their babies can be born deaf, blind, or with other disabilities.

Scientist Maurice Hilleman took a leading role developing vaccines for measles, mumps, and rubella.

These vaccines need to be effective *and* safe. One without the other is not good enough!

By 1969, Hilleman had successfully created vaccines for all three viruses. Two years later, he created the combined measles, mumps, and rubella (MMR) vaccine.

Hilleman created more than 40 vaccines over his career. His work saved more lives than that of any other scientist throughout the 1900s.

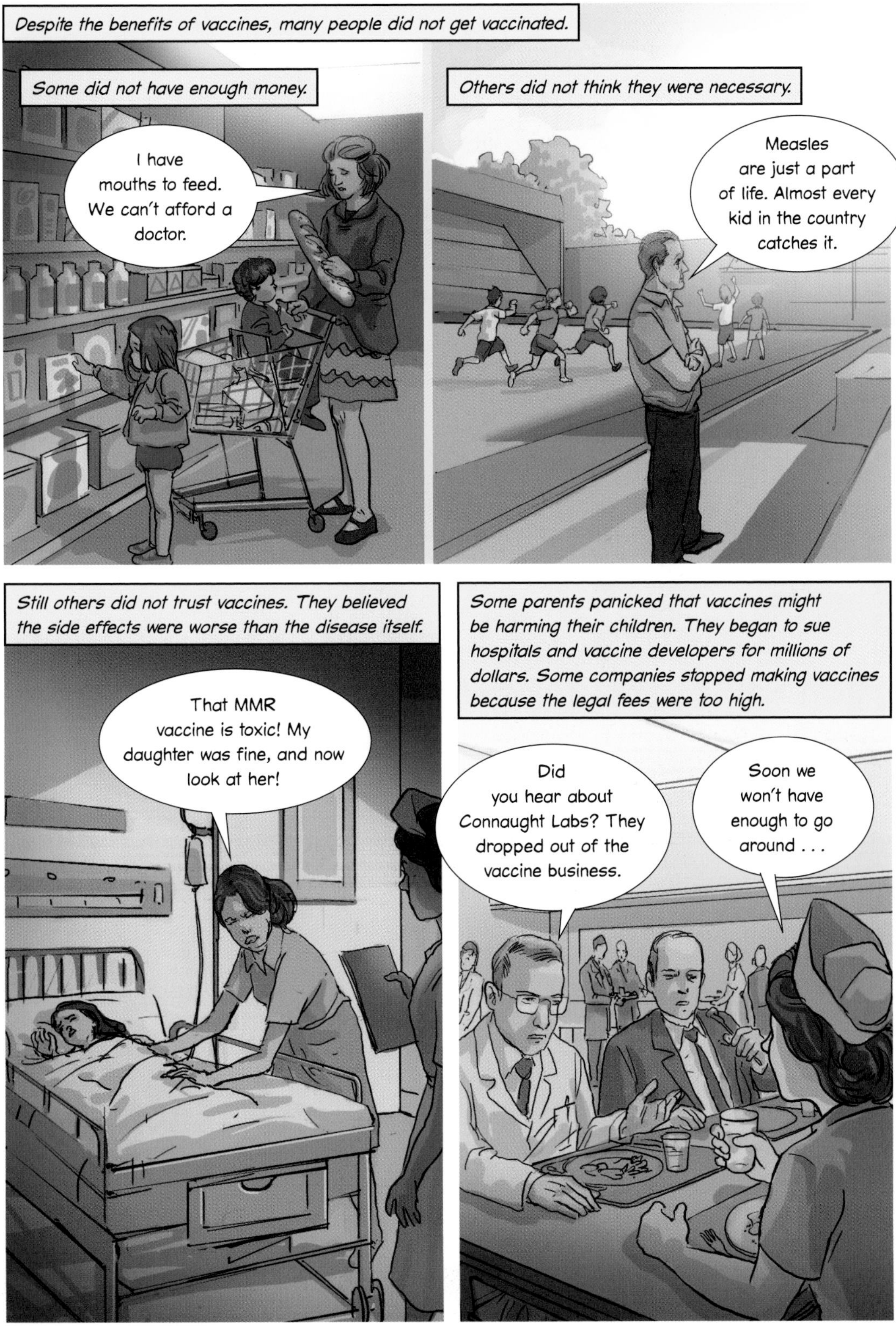
Despite the benefits of vaccines, many people did not get vaccinated.
Some did not have enough money.
I have mouths to feed. We can't afford a doctor.
Others did not think they were necessary.
Measles are just a part of life. Almost every kid in the country catches it.
Still others did not trust vaccines. They believed the side effects were worse than the disease itself.
That MMR vaccine is toxic! My daughter was fine, and now look at her!
Some parents panicked that vaccines might be harming their children. They began to sue hospitals and vaccine developers for millions of dollars. Some companies stopped making vaccines because the legal fees were too high.
Did you hear about Connaught Labs? They dropped out of the vaccine business.
Soon we won't have enough to go around . . .

CHAPTER 4: THE BATTLE FOR VACCINES

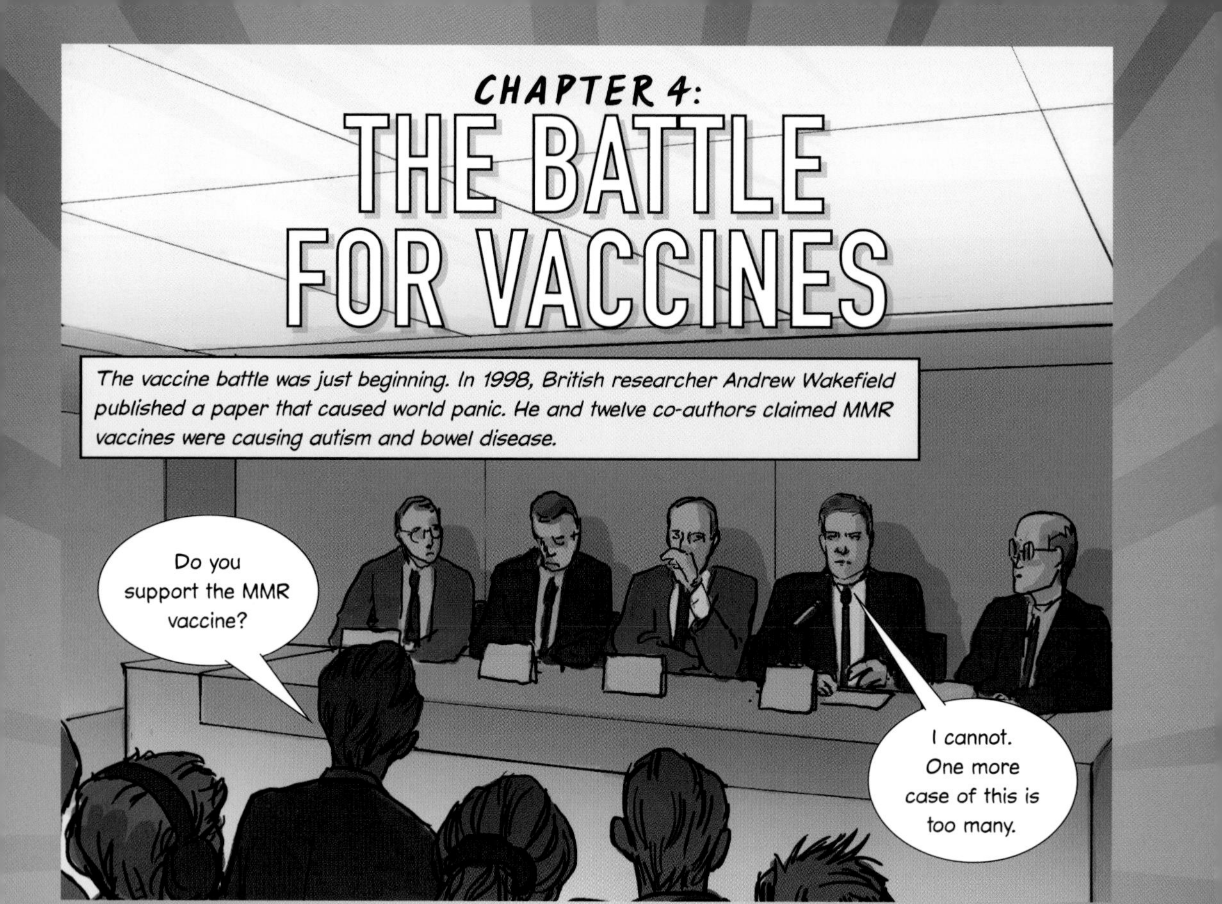

The vaccine battle was just beginning. In 1998, British researcher Andrew Wakefield published a paper that caused world panic. He and twelve co-authors claimed MMR vaccines were causing autism and bowel disease.
Do you support the MMR vaccine?
I cannot. One more case of this is too many.

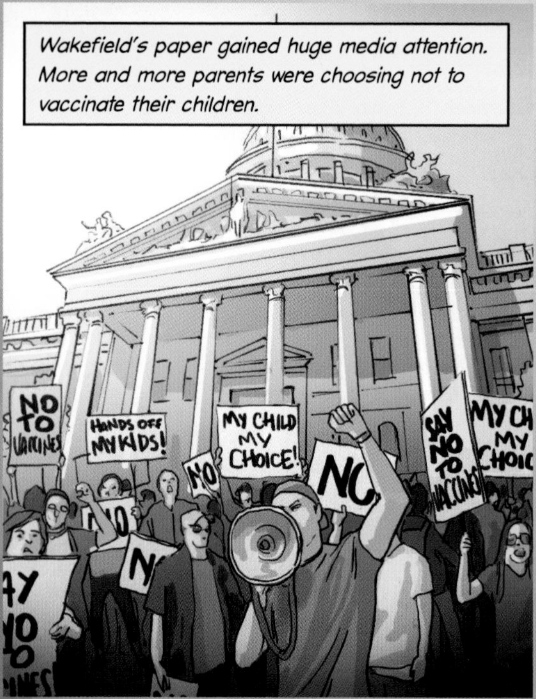

Wakefield's paper gained huge media attention. More and more parents were choosing not to vaccinate their children.
NO TO VACCINES
HANDS OFF MY KIDS!
MY CHILD MY CHOICE!
NO
SAY NO TO VACCINES

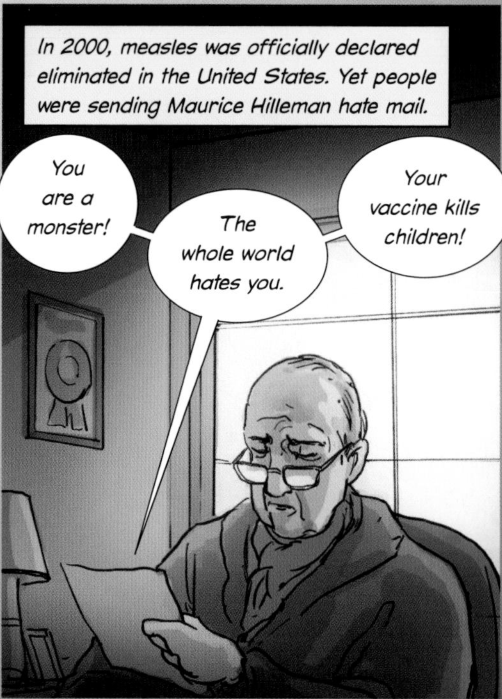

In 2000, measles was officially declared eliminated in the United States. Yet people were sending Maurice Hilleman hate mail.
You are a monster!
The whole world hates you.
Your vaccine kills children!

In 2004, journalist Brian Deer revealed that Wakefield's study had been biased from the start. Earlier, a lawyer named Richard Barr had approached Wakefield, hoping to sue MMR vaccine developers on behalf of a parent group. Both men expected to profit from the study's results.

Other scientists tested Wakefield's claims. But they found no evidence to support him.

What a scam!

Wakefield was charged with professional misconduct. The United Kingdom's General Medical Council investigated him from July 2007 to 2010.

Your research was not honest. It was not responsible. You did not care about the pain these children might suffer.

Wakefield lost his medical license.

New diseases keep vaccine developers alert. In April 2009, the H1N1 virus (swine flu) broke out in North America. Two months later, the World Health Organization (WHO) declared an H1N1 pandemic.

Flu vaccine developers began designing a new formula for H1N1. But the H1N1 virus grew slowly in the lab. This and manufacturing complications slowed down vaccine production.

By March 2010, H1N1 had killed 12,000 people and hospitalized another 250,000 in the United States.

Eventually, the WHO shipped 78 million doses of the H1N1 vaccine to 77 different countries. The pandemic ended in August 2010. It had caused up to 575,000 total deaths.

We all lament how long it took for a vaccine to be made.

The H1N1 outbreak reminded people how important vaccines are in tackling disease.

In 2001, Canada's National Microbiology Laboratory began conducting studies into a vaccine for the deadly Ebola virus.

An Ebola vaccine absolutely needs to be available for emergency use in the future.

Thirteen years later, in March 2014, the WHO reported an Ebola virus outbreak in Guinea, West Africa. It spread quickly.

By the height of the Guinea outbreak, Canadian scientists had developed enough of the vaccine to send the WHO one thousand doses.

If you have had contact with an Ebola patient, we will vaccinate you and your contacts. This should stop the virus from spreading and protect anyone in its path.

The vaccine was a success! In June 2016, the epidemic ended.

In December 2019, hospital staff came across a new virus in the city of Wuhan, China.

The virus caused the disease COVID-19 and was highly contagious. Most people recovered from COVID-19 with mild symptoms. But the virus caused life-threatening respiratory problems in a small portion of those infected.

COVID-19 spread across the world, infecting millions of people. During this time, scientists worked around the clock to develop a vaccine.

In December 2020, drug companies Pfizer and Moderna were the first to release approved vaccines.

Once again, a vaccine saved thousands, maybe millions, of lives.

SOURCE NOTES

21   Global Citizen, "Could You Patent the Sun?" YouTube video,
0:01, January 29, 2013, https://www.youtube.com
/watch?v=erHXKP386Nk.

24   Seth Mnookin, "MMR Vaccine Scare: Andrew Wakefield's
Fraudulent Study," *The Daily Beast*, January 13, 2011,
https://www.thedailybeast.com/mmr-vaccine-scare
-andrew-wakefields-fraudulent-study.

26   Maggie Fox, "Biggest Swine Flu Regret for U.S.: Vaccine
Chaos," *Reuters*, March 5, 2010, https://www.reuters
.com/article/us-flu-lessons/biggest-swine-flu-regret-for
-u-s-vaccine-chaos-idUSTRE6244LN20100305.

GLOSSARY

autism: a developmental disorder that may affect physical, social, and language skills

bacteria: a type of germ that sometimes causes disease in humans

biased: favoring certain ideas or outcomes over others

contamination: the infecting or dirtying of an object or area

disability: a physical or mental limitation

donor: a person who donates blood or an organ

embryo: an animal in its early stage of development

epidemic: an outbreak of a disease that affects a specific population or region

influenza: a virus known as the flu that causes disease in humans

inoculate: to introduce a live germ into a person's body so they create antibodies. This process is called inoculation.

leech: a type of bloodsucking worm sometimes used to treat illness in humans

pandemic: a disease that spreads over a wide area and infects many people

paralyze: to lose the ability to move

patent: a legal document that confirms ownership of an object or idea

placenta: an organ through which a mother passes nutrients to her unborn child

professional misconduct: behavior that goes against what is expected from a job or professional role

pustule: a raised area of skin containing pus

sue: to take a complaint or other legal issue to court

virus: a type of germ that sometimes causes disease in humans

FURTHER INFORMATION

Britannica Kids—Epidemic
https://kids.britannica.com/kids/article/epidemic/432953

The College of Physicians of Philadelphia: The History of Vaccines
https://www.historyofvaccines.org/timeline/all

Doeden, Matt. *The COVID-19 Pandemic: A Coronavirus Timeline*. Minneapolis: Lerner Publications, 2021.

KidsHealth—Immunizations
https://kidshealth.org/en/teens/immunizations.html

Marshall, Linda Elovitz. *The Polio Pioneer: Dr. Jonas Salk and the Polio Vaccine*. New York: Alfred A. Knopf, 2020.

Rooney, Anne. *You Wouldn't Want to Live Without Vaccinations!* New York: Franklin Watts, 2015.

INDEX